# My Family Tree

## Taken to the Grave

by

Shari Klosterman

# COPYRIGHT

Print ISBN: 9798799748692

Written by Shari Klosterman
Instagram www.instagram/familytree_takentothegrave

Editing and Book Design by Nita Robinson, *Nita Helping Hand?*
www.NitaHelpingHand.com
Cover by Kelly Martin, KAM Designs www.KAM.Design

# TABLE OF CONTENTS

COPYRIGHT 2

DEDICATION 5

INTRODUCTION 6

THE BEGINNING 7

MY EARLY YEARS 16

MOM AND I 25

FAMILY TREES AND A DNA KIT 39

THE MYSTERY GETS DEEPER 50

WHAT THE…? 55

THE SEARCH IS ON… 60

DIGGING AND MORE DIGGING 64

STARTING A NEW JOURNEY 67

GENEALOGY LESSONS 70

PUZZLE PIECES 73

QUESTIONS AND ANSWERS 77

COINCIDENCES? 85

ALL ABOUT FAMILY, NEW AND OLD 93

FIRST IMPRESSIONS 100

NEW BRANCHES AND NEW BEGINNINGS 107

A FINAL CHAPTER – BUT NOT THE END… 111

ABOUT THE AUTHOR 119

# DEDICATION

There are many people who needed to be given credit for helping me with the creation of this book.  First to my husband Ed, whose encouragement made me believe I could even do such a thing. To my daughter Ashley, who's always been supportive of this entire journey in my family discovery. To my dear friend Patty who gave me so much help in the beginning - a special thank you. Lastly, to my parents and my entire family - for who this book is for. None of this would have been possible without you.

Much love,

Shari

# INTRODUCTION

I feel like I am like a lot of people. I wanted to see what my DNA said about my family and learn about our health history, if possible. Doing a family tree, I assumed, would be enjoyable. I wanted to see how far back I could go and discover if there were some well-known people in our tree. I had no idea what I was about to discover…

In late 2016, I took a DNA test through 23andMe. I thought this would be cool; acquire some fascinating actualities about myself and learn more about my family's health history. Both of my parents had passed on (Dad in 1973 and Mom in 2011), so while I did know some things regarding my family history, I wanted to learn all I could.

# THE BEGINNING

Mom, Dad and me, 1961

My story began in Louisville, Kentucky in March of 1961. I was the sixth and last child of Charles and Mary Wells. I was given the name Shari Lynn, named after the ventriloquist, Shari Lewis. I have five older siblings; Wilbur, Nancy, Barbara (who died at birth), Michael (Mike) and

Daniel (Dan). There is quite a bit of age difference between me and the oldest – about 22 years, and about ten and a half years between Dan and me. My oldest brother and sister were already gone from home when I was born.

I've been married to my husband Ed (Eddie) since 2010. I have a daughter, Ashley, from a previous marriage, and he has a daughter, Anastasia, as well as identical twin sons, Andrew and Alexander from his previous marriage. Between us we now have five beautiful grandchildren from ages 1 to 13. My husband just retired from a large auto manufacturing company and I still work as a payroll accountant. I love watching college football or basketball and cheering hard for the Cardinals! I've been a bowler almost my entire life, and you can find me in a bowling center a few nights a week – and a tournament or two throughout the year. I also play the flute and have started learning photography.

Dad, Anthony, Wilbur, Willie Lee and Gene

My dad, Charles (1915-1973), was originally from Clarkson, Kentucky. Dad was one of seven children; five boys and two girls. Geneva and Edna – then Dad, Anthony, Wilbur, Willie and Gene. I never met my paternal grandparents, but in what little research I had done, I learned that my grandfather died when Dad was about 17, and my grandmother remarried but died in a car accident about two years before I was born.

I did know most of my aunts and uncles though. Uncle Anthony, who was just a few years younger than Dad, had served in the Navy during WWII. He was one of the 1,177 that were killed on the USS Arizona when it was attacked on December 7, 1941, such a horrible time in our nation's history. I can remember it was never talked about. Mom would tear up just thinking about it. For many years it was thought that he was still in the Pacific, entombed in the ship, but years later, after I started the family tree, I learned that he had in fact been recovered and was buried at the National Cemetery in Honolulu. I have yet to visit the USS Arizona Memorial but have had friends take pictures for me. To see his name on that wall – I can only imagine what it would be like to see it in person. It's on my bucket list to visit one day.

My mom, Mary (1919-2011), came from a small town called Walton, Indiana, literally a blip on a map. The interesting thing is that Mom never had a birth certificate – she said the doctor in that town just never made one out. How weird that seemed to me at the time.

Mom was the oldest of four. Two brothers, Robert and Paul, and a half-sister, Phyllis (Phyl). I knew my maternal grandparents. My grandmother, Grace, was married twice. I only met my biological grandfather once, I think. Mom had traveled to Florida when I was a teen to visit him. I don't think they had a strong relationship, but I never really knew why. My grandmother's second husband, Aunt Phyl's dad, is the one that I always thought of as my grandfather.

Mom's baby picture

Mom in her early 20s

Mom and Dad in the early years

My grandmother, who was born in 1901, lived to be 91. She was feisty and strict! But I guess when you grow up in some of the worst times of the 20th century, you learn to survive. As a kid, while we were there visiting, it was dinner time and I didn't like what was for dinner. Grandma," I said," You're in trouble!"

"Why is that?" she asked.

"I don't like what you're fixing for dinner!"

She looked at me with that look she had. "I'm not in trouble – you are!" I didn't eat much that night!

Dad had come to Louisville to find work in the mid-1930s. Mom, at 17, came to visit her dad in Louisville in 1936. While here in Louisville, she went to the local high school for her senior year. During this time, her stepmother became ill. With only six weeks of school remaining, she quit to take care of her. She knew she was needed at home, so that's what she did. That was her character. I think she really hated the fact that she didn't have a high school diploma, but she was one of the smartest people I was blessed to know. During this time is when she met my dad and they began dating. When the summer was over, she was supposed to go back to Indiana and work on the farm. I remember Mom saying she wasn't having any of that. So, she stayed in Louisville, and she and Dad were married about six weeks later. Grandma was NOT happy about that at all.

Mom was determined to stay in the big city. They lived above a grocery store in the west end of town. In the spring of 1937, the rains came for days. The Ohio River spilled its banks deep into the city of Louisville, and Mom and Dad retreated to the country (Clarkson) for several weeks. Times were hard and I think they stayed in the country for several months.

My two oldest siblings were born at home. There were not many hospitals down in the country back in those days. Of my siblings, two of my brothers (Wilbur and Mike), have passed away. My sister Nancy lives in North Carolina, and my brother Dan lives here in Louisville.

All 5 siblings – circa 1967

# MY EARLY YEARS

I guess you could say I was painstakingly labeled the late-in-life child. Dad was 45 and Mom was 41 when I was born. Mom would talk about how she believed she was done having children, but then I showed up. My brothers and sister would tease me about how I was doted on a bit more than the others. As a little girl, I frequently tagged along with Dad. I loved that too. When Dad went someplace, I was the shadow that followed along. I learned how to fish (caught a nice catfish on a cane pole!), gig a frog (really, I just held the flashlight), and when I was younger, I would go to the beer depot with Dad. I would drink root beer while he gulped down the fermented ones.

I had my brothers and sisters, but I always felt like I was an only child since it was just the three of us so much. There was always a special connection between Dad and me. Maybe because I was the youngest, I don't know, but I can just remember as a kid that whenever the opportunity presented itself, I was with him.

Dad, who was a smoker, also had a problem with alcohol. His brothers, from what I recall, all had issues with it as well. He was not known to be abusive in any way, but he always had a drink of some kind in his hand whether it was beer or, later in life, whiskey. I later learned that while he was a good breadwinner, he was not the best husband to Mom. My sister had told me how Dad was never home and Mom was left many times to take care of things around the house. Many nights were of him coming in smashed from some bar and falling on his way to find the bedroom to go sleep it off. All of this was before I came along. Years later, I remember as a kid how we were at a family reunion and Dad fell out of a folding chair. Dad was tall – about 6'2" – and as a young kid, seeing him take a tumble really terrified me. Alcohol would pretty much consume his day if he didn't have a job to go to. He was a maintenance mechanic for a local chemical company, a job he had for many years.

Dad and me

Dad, Mom, Nancy, Danny and me Circa 1965

When I was about four, we moved to a new house. That home became the house I and everyone else grew to know and love. Shortly after the move, Dad suffered a heart attack. The doctors told him he needed to quit drinking the beer (but said nothing about the smoking), so he gave whiskey a try.

Mom and Dad did enjoy some things together though, and really took a liking to hunting and fishing. In fact, they joined a place nearby where they could fish any time they wanted. Many weekends were spent fishing there, and it's where I caught my whopper catfish on the cane pole. I was probably eight or nine at the time. That fish seemed like a monster! Here is a picture of me holding that fish, looking like I had just caught a big fin tuna out of the ocean. Mom even caught a snapping turtle once. She took her first and only attempt to make turtle soup… oh how awful that was!

During this time, they found a nice little cabin for sale on the Kentucky River in Carrollton, Kentucky. We spent many weekends there fishing, swimming, and boating on the river. I remember Dad had lines of different lengths on the dock to see where the fish were biting. I can remember seeing one moving fast, so I pulled it up. To my surprise, there was what I thought was a snake right there staring right at me! It turned out to be an eel, and Mom and Dad had a great laugh about that. To this day, I avoid swimming in a river or lake. It was an enjoyable time there, and many family members would come often to stay the weekend. They named the place Camp Chamadana, named mainly after Dad, Mom, Nancy, and Dan as they all had helped in getting the place.

Mom fancy fishing!

My childhood was a good one. I guess you could say we were like any other family. It was the late 60s so Dad worked and Mom did everything else. Mom wasn't really associated with any church or religion at the time, but Dad was Catholic. All my siblings attended Catholic grade school, and Dan had graduated from a Catholic High School. I can remember going to Mass with Dad and Dan as a little girl. Dad had taken a liking to the Priest who had been directing mass, so after he left the church for another parish, so did we.

When it came time for me to start school, the church had a lower school attendance, so they eliminated first and second grades. When third grade came around, although I could now register with any of the Catholic schools, Mom was not a fan of me leaving the public school system since I was doing exceptionally well, so I stayed there. I was the only child that didn't make my first communion or attend a Catholic school at some point in my education. It wasn't until I was much older that I went back to church and made my confirmation into the Catholic faith.

In March of 1973, barely a week after my 12th birthday, Dad left for work that afternoon. He worked a swing shift at the chemical plant so every week or so his schedule would change. Mom got a phone call that afternoon that changed her life. Mom was told that she needed to go to the hospital. I was sent to a friend's house so I wouldn't be home alone. Soon after Dad arrived at work, he suffered another heart attack and had fallen down a flight of stairs. Sadly, this one he didn't survive. I can remember my brother coming to tell me that Dad had passed away. How was this even possible? What would I do without my dad? I just couldn't comprehend that he wasn't coming home anymore. I felt so empty. Even though I was only 12, I understood what had happened. What was going to happen to me and Mom? So many people showed up to the house. Mom was so distraught. I had never seen her cry like that. I can't remember if I cried, but I remember how lonely I felt. It was so surreal for Dad not to be around anymore.

I remember going back to school, and how it felt when my friends and classmates didn't understand what I was feeling inside. They all had their dads, but I didn't. It was all so strange to me. Teachers were there to help, but I felt like it was all a dream… but it wasn't. Just like that Dad was gone. It was an emptiness I had never felt or experienced before.

After some time had passed, Mom gave all of us kids something that had belonged to Dad. Dad had a belt buckle that he had received from work for his 25 years of service. The belt buckle had a small diamond in it so Mom took that diamond out and had a ring made for me that I still have today. I still wear it on occasion as a memory of the Dad I had for 12 years. Twelve years wasn't a very long time, and I always wondered what it would have been like had he lived longer and had been around while I grew up. But I had great memories with him and I'll hold those memories in my heart forever. One day I will pass along the ring that had been given to me as a little girl.

# MOM AND I

After Dad died, it was just Mom and I. All my siblings were pretty much married and gone. Growing up without Dad was strange at first. Fortunately, Mom had just gotten her driver's license about a year before Dad passed. She took lessons to learn to drive as a surprise to my dad. She was so excited to show him that she had her license! She later learned that he actually knew she was taking lessons, so not quite the surprise she had thought. She drove that car until well into her eighties before Mom decided she didn't need to drive anymore (she had just quit bowling too), so my brother helped her sell it. It was a 1972 American Motors Hornet. I don't think it even had 50,000 miles on it when it was sold.

Mom didn't really work much while she was raising me and my siblings, which I guess was typical for that time. Only after I was born did she decide to venture out into the workforce. A couple that lived across the street from where my parents lived at the time (mid 1950s) introduced Mom to bowling. There was a center up the street from us, Poplar Level Lanes, and she joined a league there. It wasn't even a mile from where they lived at the time, so the convenience of being close made it easier. After a few years of bowling in leagues, she decided to work there. She became a secretary for many leagues and tournaments, and ended up starting youth leagues and teaching kids how to bowl. Back in those days, if you were a secretary for a bowling league, you kept all records on paper. Every week I remember her writing down each individual league member's scores, adding to the previous week for a total, then dividing by the number of games to get that person's average. All of this was done without a calculator. Her math skills were amazing. She did this for over 20 years.

Mom continued to bowl for many years until her hip started giving her trouble and she eventually had a hip replacement. With over 50 years of bowling experience, she loved her senior's leagues, enjoyed being with her friends, and always enjoyed a beer when she bowled too.

Mom was such an independent woman and coming to the realization that she couldn't do things like she used to was frustrating for her. In 1997, Mom was inducted into the Louisville Women's Bowling Association Hall of Fame for her many years of service and working with young children, teaching them how to bowl. That was such a thrill for her. She was just in awe the whole night. To see her up there receiving her award was wonderful, and we were all so happy and proud of her. My oldest brother, who lived in Arizona, flew in, and her sister had surprised her too. Seeing that smile on her face, I knew it would be a night she would never forget.

Mom dated a few people over the years, but never remarried. I hated that she never found anyone after Dad. She loved to do stuff and that just wasn't something Dad was into. They would hardly go out to a restaurant as Dad thought it was wasteful to spend money to eat out. I never really saw them go anywhere together, so for Mom to bowl and work at the center gave her something to be involved in. Mom was a people-person; not overly extroverted, but just genuinely liked people.

At about six weeks of age, I was at the bowling center with her. I think all my siblings at some point in their life bowled youth and/or adult leagues. My oldest brother even sat pins at the bowling center before electric pinsetters were around. Years later, trophies adorned the wall at home from all her years of bowling. She loved to bowl, and I think it was something that gave her great enjoyment.

When I was about 8 years old I began youth leagues there then moved up to adult leagues. Mom was my coach, but my stubborn self didn't really want to pay much attention. I was a lefty, and everyone else around me was right-handed. I wanted to be like everyone else! It made me feel like I wasn't doing it correctly because I was left-handed. Why did I have to stand on the "left" side of the lane?

At 60, it's still a big part of my life. I have her to thank for that. I love the sport and I've been blessed to have had some success in my bowling career. Two perfect games, some local and state tournament wins, trips all over the country, and being inducted into our local and state Hall of Fames. I would always call and let Mom know how my league night went or how I did in a tournament.

I also followed in her footsteps, coaching a high school team for nine years. It was the same school that my daughter later attended. Ashley was on the team for a few of those years. In 2009, my girls team won the state championship. Our team wasn't necessarily the strongest amongst all the teams, but I knew we had what it would take to win. We had worked hard all season and put it all together that weekend. I was so proud of those girls. Winning that was one of the proudest moments of my own bowling career.

When Mom was very young, she lived in South Bend, Indiana. She really loved singing. In fact, she sang on the radio during her time there. Mom had a beautiful soprano voice. Music was always a staple in the house when I was growing up. She had taught herself to play the organ, and had a stereo and many albums that she would play and sing to. Nancy and Mom would sing beautiful duets together.

She also loved her gardening and would knit and crochet a great deal. She had two sewing machines; she even made a wedding dress for one of the granddaughters, and for many years she did alterations. People from all over would hear of Mary and her alterations. You name it, she made it or altered it! All the kids and most of the grandkids have something that she had made from her knitting or crocheting. She tried to show me how to knit or crochet multiple times, but I could never get the hang of it. It seemed so awkward for me to do. As I look back I can see how she loved us all so very much in her own special way.

Mom suffered by losing two children during her lifetime. She lost her son Mike back in 2005. Mike had been diabetic since his early twenties, and around 1992 he was the recipient of a double organ transplant. His kidneys had been failing – and had been doing dialysis three times a week for several years. His doctor realized that the recipients' pancreas would match as well so a new pancreas and kidney gave him the chance to have a more normal life again.

Mom's 80th birthday... one of the last pictures of all of us together

Technically, Mike was no longer a diabetic, but diabetes is such a debilitating disease that it caused him some horrible issues even after the transplant. He suffered terribly with strokes, but he was a man of strong faith and never gave up. In March of 2005, he suffered another stroke, and after several days in the hospital he passed away.

For a parent to lose a child; I could not imagine the pain Mom suffered. I didn't think she would make it through the funeral. It was his illness that got me interested in genealogy. Then, so very unexpectedly, she lost her oldest, Wilbur, who died in November of 2010 of a pulmonary embolism. I had to be the one to tell her that he had passed, and that was without a doubt the worst thing I have ever had to do. I was just brokenhearted watching Mom's grief. He lived in Arizona and she couldn't travel so she was forced to mourn him from home. I believe her losing her oldest child in 2010 really hit her hard and I felt that started a decline with her health and her life.

After Wilbur's passing, that Thanksgiving and Christmas were really difficult. It made me reflect upon myself, and seeing how this had affected her and me. She had lost her husband and two sons, and I've lost my dad and two brothers. Wilbur and I, even though he was the oldest and lived in Arizona, were pretty close and spoke on the phone a lot. I realized how I saw my own life, as I'm almost 50, and wondered where all the time had gone.

Up until that time, Mom had pretty much been a healthy person. She took medications for a few things, but for being 92, her health was pretty good. Her mother had lived to be 91, and my hopes are that "I got some of those good genes". In November of 2011, she went to the hospital for an ulcer that had been giving her some discomfort. Two days before she was to leave, she had a mild heart attack which was a surprise to all of us. Mom had never had any heart issues before. The doctor spoke to us and told us that it was mild and there wasn't a lot of heart damage. He let us know that she would be able to go back home and live comfortably, she just needed to take it easy. I stayed that night at the hospital, and she awoke to see me there.

"Did I have a heart attack?" she asked.

"You sure did," I told her. It wasn't anything very serious, and I told her that she'd be staying a couple more days then she could go home after they did some tests. She went back to sleep, but after that she didn't ever really seem like herself.

Some of the grandkids had come by to visit her, but she didn't seem up to talking much. Just a few words and a smile here and there was about it. A few days later, I called early in the morning to check on her and the nurse told me she was comfortable but didn't really want to eat much. Dan was on his way up there as he would go during the day and I went in the evenings. About 20 minutes after I had called the hospital, her doctor called me to say that he was so sorry, but my mom had passed away. I couldn't believe it. Mom was 92 years old, but even at 92, we all thought she was going to go home. It was such a shock. The void of her not being there hurt my heart greatly. I sat in my office at work until Eddie came to pick me up since I couldn't even drive, and we went up to the hospital. Dan and Trish arrived, then Ashley arrived a short time later. We all held her hands and just cried. I think that was the first time I had seen my brother cry. It was just so heartbreaking.

In the meantime, Nancy had been traveling up here to visit with Mom, and she had called while I was on my way to the hospital. I didn't want to answer the phone, and I didn't want to upset her while she drove. I never want to give that kind of news over the phone. She called back again, and I finally answered… but it was like she already knew. I can't imagine how long that drive must have seemed.

We know we don't have forever with our parents, but it's still such a shock. I couldn't believe she was gone; it was like a part of me was gone too. We all miss Mom greatly and remember her strong will and caring nature. In addition to her kids, she had 21 grandchildren, 18 great-grandchildren, and six great-great grandchildren.

# FAMILY TREES AND A DNA KIT

It was around 2008 or 2009, before Mom passed away, that I first thought about building a family tree. I used the site called My Heritage. Mom was helpful, as she'd had a family tree given to her by her brother-in-law. This was helpful in filling in some blanks with names of people I didn't know. It was truly enjoyable seeing things piece together. I had a couple of generations of family, not really a lot, but it was still something to have and to pass down to the next generation.

While doing my research, I came upon some interesting information. When cross-referencing names that showed up from other family history trees, I thought I found a link to my great-grandmother. Her maiden name was Wagoner, and while there were many ways of spelling that name, it appeared that I had found her. Using other website links that were available, I was able to go back another eight generations. Although different spellings made it somewhat challenging, I felt pretty confident that I had made some headway in this part of the family tree. Much to my surprise, one of the names that showed up had a picture attached. As I dug deeper down this part of the tree, I discovered that my 7th generation grandfather was a personal bodyguard of General George Washington during the Revolutionary War! Well, this is a neat find, I told myself, but wondered I if this was true. While doing all this research, you wonder if what you find is factual or if it's other people's guesses that you're seeing. Nothing looked out of sorts, but I wanted to see if I could find more.

A year or two later, Eddie and I were taking a summer vacation. We mainly drove around the state to places we had never visited before. While he was driving, I was back to finding out about the Wagoner side of the family tree. I came across a newspaper article from a town in northern Ohio that told about someone who had done a family history of the Wagoner name. I told Eddie it was just a few hours drive, and asked if we could go up there. I was so intrigued by the information I was reading that we took a day trip and drove to Fremont, Ohio.

According to the article, there were artifacts stored at the Rutherford B. Hayes Presidential Library which, we learned after we got there, was the first Presidential Library ever built. I explained to them that I thought I might be a direct descendant of the Wagner family. After talking to several people who worked at the library and asking them about the John Wagoner name, we were surprised by a curator of the library who came up to us and asked us point blank, "Are you the ones asking about John Wagoner?"

I was surprised but said yes, not knowing who this person was. At that point the gentleman said, "Oh, he's a big deal around here!" The curator proceeded to tell us about him. They brought out a book that had been written with all the names, different spellings, and a family tree of the Wagoner descendants. The book was written in the early 1940's, well before my time, but there in print was my family! I was so shocked to find that listed in this book were my grandmother, mother and even my oldest brother's names, and I was able to trace back directly to him. I was excited to say that I was a direct descendant of the man who helped protect our soon-to be first President of the United States.

The curator at the library showed us artifacts that General Washington gave to my grandfather and the other bodyguards as a thank-you for saving his life. With white gloves on, we were able to see and hold an axe and a walking cane/saber that had belonged to my grandfather. I learned that the book that was written was online and I could purchase a copy for myself.

The curator told us that he was buried in a cemetery close by. What a great surprise that was! They were gracious enough to give us directions to the cemetery. Once there, we found his grave, and the stone for him was incredible. It included many flags and a SAR (Sons of the American Revolution) medallion. What a great honor it was to stand there, knowing that he was my great grandfather. That trip turned out to be such an exciting and wonderful learning experience for both Eddie and me.

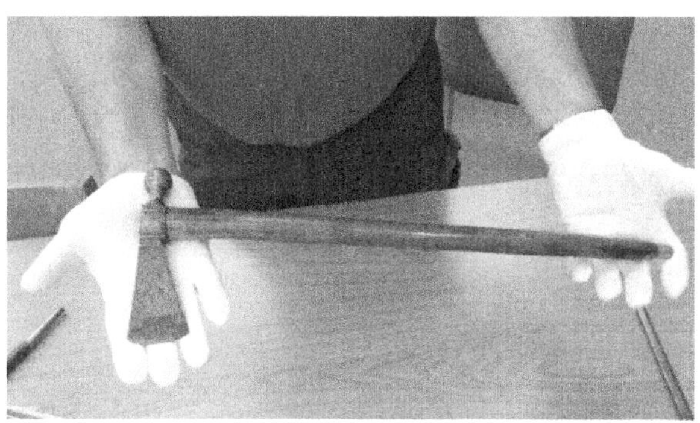

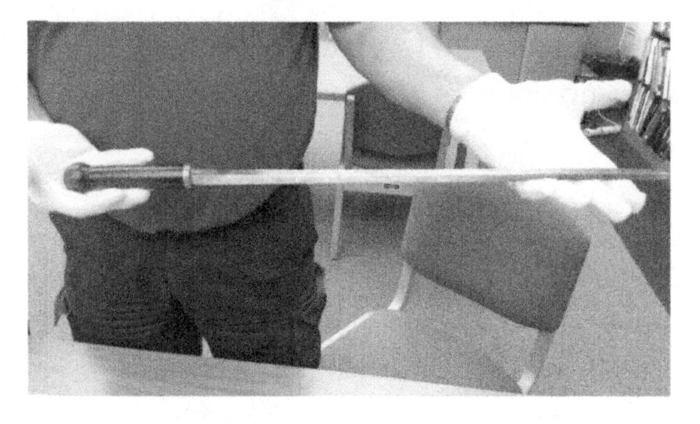

A few years after (Mom had passed by this time) building this family tree, I thought that if I did a DNA test, I could get a lot more history about where our family had started, seeing what countries our ancestors came from, what percentages, as well as a health history. Eddie was curious as to why I wanted to know about my medical history. I told him that I thought it would be beneficial to me and other family members to have that knowledge. In 2015-2016, I decided to order my DNA kit from 23andMe, and after a few weeks it arrived. I added my spit to a test tube and waited six to eight weeks before I finally saw my results. The health traits were interesting. Eddie and I went over the results and were quite surprised at how closely they matched up to me.

There were things I expected, with no real surprises. Things like, did you know it's a genetic trait to smell an odor from asparagus when you go to the bathroom? or that people who don't like cilantro might think it tastes like soap. I have a blood disorder that is apparently genetic (I had a severe hemorrhage when Ashley was born), and I was hoping more information might show up, telling me which side of the family it came from since I never really knew. I figured it might be Dad's side of the family since they were all deceased and, as far as I knew, Mom's side of the family didn't have anything like that. Nothing showed up in relation to the blood disorder, and that was a little disappointing, but it is very interesting to find out the things that the results show you.

When you get your results, it passes along a list of people whose DNA matches you. I would go back and look periodically to see whose DNA I matched up to. This wasn't the main reason I ordered the kit; I was more curious about where our family originated, as well as the health part of it. Also, I didn't really know of any other family members out there who had taken a test, so I wasn't sure whose names I might recognize and whose I might not.

After looking at my DNA matches, I didn't really see anyone that sounded familiar. However, I did see that I had a match with someone in Louisiana. I thought that was strange since we don't have any relatives in Louisiana that I knew about. The person I matched to in Louisiana (female) I shared about 10.5% DNA with. I was asking myself if that was a big percentage or not. I really didn't know what the numbers meant. I saw further down the list that there were a few people who matched around two percent or slightly more. Still, the names didn't sound familiar. How is it that I shared DNA with people I'd never heard of?

Like the other DNA sites, you can message people through the site so I thought maybe these people were some distant relatives way down the line, and maybe I could find a similar surname that we matched to. At the time it wasn't a big deal; I knew who my family was, so I really didn't think much about it. I just thought it was a bit strange that I had never heard of any of these people before.

Some months later, I noticed that I had a message from someone. It was the lady in Louisiana named Mary Lou. She told me she was from Louisiana and that her parents were from there as well. She gave me a list of surnames, but none that sounded familiar at all. We tried to make a connection with names, but never could find a name that would match between us. That was September of 2017.

I had spoken to my sister Nancy about all this. Since she's 20 years older, I thought maybe she knew of something I didn't know about. Nancy said she didn't really know anything specific but that Mom and Dad didn't have such a great relationship years back before I was born. He and Mom would argue a lot more than they should. Then Nancy said to me," Well, I wonder if Dad has some offspring out there that we don't know about!" She really thought that could be a possibility given the history of his frequent absences from home. Then it became a bit of a mystery, thinking we might have relatives out there that we never knew about! We both kind of laughed about it and I said, "You hear about this sort of thing more and more all the time." We wondered how we could figure out how to trace any of this back to people that Dad might have known and draw a connection there. I told Nancy that so much time had passed, and we wondered if there were any other relatives that could be living anywhere.

I wanted to see if I could get any male family members to do the DNA test. I thought if there was some male DNA for our family tree, it might possibly help piece things together.

I contacted my brother Dan to see if he would be willing to do a DNA test. He didn't really want to do that so I told him that it was fine, no big deal. I reached out to my nephew Mike, and told him what I was doing and how I was looking for a male family member to submit DNA. He said sure, he would do it. I sent him the link to the website to get the test. I figured the more male DNA I had to build on our family tree, the more accurate it would be.

A few weeks went by, and Mike told me he got his results back. I went to my account, and sure enough, there was his name and our DNA connections and percentages. I remember laughing and saying that we're a match as he and I shared 12% DNA. Since his dad (my brother

Mike) had been Type 1 diabetic for most of his life, I thought the DNA test might shed some light on that, possibly showing any traits for that disease, especially for any grandchildren in my brother's family. I did think it was kind of odd that my nephew and I shared 12% and some lady in Louisiana and I shared over 10.5% – someone I didn't even know!

I called Nancy and told her about how Mike, Jr. had taken the test and how he got his results and what all it showed. She also became intrigued about the whole thing. She wondered what it would be like if she took one. I laughed and said, "Well, it will probably be really similar to mine!"

# THE MYSTERY GETS DEEPER

I mentioned having others on 23andMe that I had matched to. These matches were of a lesser percentage, so I thought maybe they could provide me with some information, like others who could be a match to anyone in our family. I hoped they could shed some light as to anyone who might have been to Kentucky or the Louisville area that we could tie back to my dad. Also, I could see on the website how people were connected, and I saw that by selecting one of those, it showed relatives we had in common. I thought this was so bizarre! Where did all these people come from that we never knew of? This helped convince me and Nancy that she was correct, that Dad had fathered some children that none of us knew anything about. This was all just mind blowing. How cool would it be to find these relatives of ours? I reached out to Mary Lou and asked her if she or any family members that she knew of might have been to Kentucky. She didn't know of anyone that had been to Kentucky but said she would ask other relatives if they might know anything.

I called Nancy back and told her the names of the people that matched my DNA. She said to me, "I really figured he had some children out there. Mom probably never knew, or if she did, she never mentioned anything like that, even after he passed away." Nancy and I talked to Dan and he didn't know anything either but agreed that given Dad's behavior it would certainly be possible. Dan is ten and a half years older than me, so between he and Nancy, they would have known a lot more information than I ever would.

I messaged a few of the people on the 23andMe site, asking about any information they could provide. Mary Lou and I talked a few times off and on. Since we couldn't find any connection and she wasn't able to find anything from other relatives, she suggested I get in touch with some of the others I had matched to. She was related to them as well and thought they might have more information than she did.

I contacted another one of my matches, a lady named Kelly, and while she didn't have any surnames that matched me, she told me to get in touch with another person on my list, a lady named Natalie. Natalie is a cousin to Mary Lou who told me she was the one who had built the family tree, and she might have a lot more information for me.

I messaged Natalie, and she was so helpful. She and I tried to match names and places that might have crossed paths, but found nothing there either. Another dead end, I thought. She was from Louisiana too, but now lived in Arizona. I told her that my oldest brother had lived there and that I still had family in Tucson. She had lived in Tucson also. She was a nurse and worked at one of the hospitals there. She told me that she had a genealogy account with Ancestry, and if it would help, she would send me a link so I could view it as a guest to see if any names possibly matched or sounded familiar.

I got on her account to start looking at names, but found nothing… a complete dead end. I was so disappointed. None of the names or places matched any thing or place around Kentucky or Indiana. Whoever might have been an offspring of Dad's didn't live around here, or I guess they had moved away. I realized it was going to be really hard to find anything. This search was going to take some intense digging, but I was willing to dig to find answers. Surely there was some connection – somewhere... There had to be, I just had to find it.

After I had my account set up with My Heritage, I found other free sites like Find a Grave and Family Search. Find a Grave is just that; pictures of gravesites at cemeteries. I thought it odd that there were people that actually go to cemeteries and take pictures of graves! It's really helpful to get those verifications for your family tree though. You can also see celebrities and other famous people's graves there.

A co-worker of mine had told me about the FamilySearch website and how you can find a lot of information on there for free. FamilySearch is a website that is run by the Church of Jesus Christ of Latter-Day Saints – The Mormon Church – and their website is good about getting all kinds of records: marriage, birth, death, baptism, census;

just about anything you could imagine. A great feature of their website is that if you have documentation to support your find, you can upload and save it. You can choose to add contact information in case anyone wants to reach you to discuss or have any questions about the information you uploaded. Knowing that you could contact someone on FamilySearch would become a valuable tool later.

I had generated what was a good start to our family tree at this point, so I would use all the resources I could to help build on it. I always went back to see if anything had changed, if any new names popped up or if there were any messages. Nothing. I told Nancy that we might have hit a dead end since nothing I had found really tied back to Dad. If there were descendants of Dad's out there, they most likely didn't have the same last name, so unless other people happened to take a DNA test, we would never really know.

I was really bummed at this point, since I had thought I might get lucky and find a connection somewhere. I wasn't giving up though… I was confident something would show up at some point. It had to!

# WHAT THE...?

By this time, it was late 2018, and after talking over the past several months and still not finding any connections anywhere, Nancy decided to go ahead and buy a DNA kit to take the test too. Not that her doing her DNA would help solve any mysteries, but she wanted to know about any medical information that could be out there about her. Her kit came, she did everything, and sent it off. Again, it normally takes six to eight weeks after it's sent back in to see the results. Her daughter and I created an account for her since she didn't have a computer at home. When her results came back, I realized that they had been uploaded so I looked at her results before I called her.

She had matches to me and, of course, to our nephew Mike. I read her health information, but there was nothing unusual there. I looked at her DNA matches and saw those results. She and Mike are around 23% matched. She and I are about 24% matched.

Wait… just 24%? That seemed odd to me. Shouldn't siblings be closer to 50%? Why are she and I only 24%?

I read further down and wondered why she and our nephew Mike, Jr. matched closer at 23.6% than he and I did at 12%?

I kept reading the results. I was so confused and didn't understand why these numbers weren't more similar to our family – why the weird differences?

Then it was as if a bolt hit me in the head. I hadn't even read down all the way. It was as if the lid of the jar had just opened with all the answers.

Oh. My. God.

I sat there in stunned silence for what seemed like forever. Was this correct? Could there be a mistake? Are DNA tests 100% accurate? What the actual hell was happening right now?

Nancy and I's predicted relationship = Half-sisters.

I was motionless. I bet I read that a million times… Half-sisters. We're *half* sisters.

Like, how? What? There MUST be some mistake! I can't remember if I cried or if I just tried to understand what I had just read. How was this even possible? It was like I was reading someone else's information.

NO. NO. NO…it was NOT possible. I kept looking at the results over and over and over, but there was no mistake.

There I sat at my computer, staring at a screen that was telling me that at 57 years old, to see with my own eyes on this 23andMe DNA website – the one that I did for fun to find our family history, our family roots – that the dad that taught me how to gig a frog, take me to drink root beer and fish… wasn't my Dad.

I lost it… I was numb, just numb. I can't even describe it. I didn't know how to feel.

I sat at that table for what seemed like hours. I was by myself at the time, and I didn't even know who to call or talk to. I just broke down. Was this some dark secret that I was never told? Did others know about this? All the questions that went through my head consumed me.

Eddie had worked the night shift and called me on his break later that night. I told him everything I had just found out. "You're not going to believe this," I said… and proceeded to tell him everything the results showed. I was inconsolable at that point. He was as stunned as I was. When he asked me if I was ok, I couldn't even answer him through the tears. I didn't know how to feel. *How could this happen? How?* That's all I could say. *How is my dad NOT my dad?* I just couldn't comprehend what was going on.

My emotions for the next few days and weeks were all over the place. How could this even be possible? I didn't know how to feel and I couldn't even talk to anyone about it. Suddenly, I felt like I was separated from everything. Sometimes I was angry, other times I was sad. *What do I do now?* I kept asking myself. Would I find out "who" this person was? Did I even want to know who this person was? This was some kind of story you might read or hear about, but I never thought it would actually be happening to me. That was as lost as I had ever felt in my entire life.

# THE SEARCH IS ON...

After a few days of trying to absorb what I had found out, I called my sister to tell her what I had learned. At first I don't think she realized what I had told her. My voice was solemn. "Nancy, your DNA test came back, and when I read the results, the DNA test says we're only half-sisters. You and I share a percentage of DNA that would only match up for half siblings. Full siblings would be closer to 50%." It was so hard just to say all that to her.

She was just as stunned as I was. "What? Are you sure?" she asked.

"Yea, the DNA is correct. You and Mike also share more DNA than he and I do. It's true. All this time we thought it was Dad who had other children out there; now we know that's not the case." We were both in a state of disbelief.

When she asked me how I felt, I answered, "I don't know how I feel, to be honest… this is all a lot to absorb. It shook me to the core, honestly." After I finished the call, I called Dan and told him what I had found out. While we were all close to Mom, Dan and she were probably a bit closer. He lived closer to her and he was always the one who could be there for her at a minute's notice. I had a really hard time telling him what I'd found out. The disbelief that was between us all was something that can't be described.

I don't remember exactly how that conversation went, but between the three of us siblings, knowing that me, the baby of the family, had a different father was something that would take some getting used to. Never in a million years did any of us believe this could be true. For several days I just tried to take it all in. I think one thing that maybe made it a little easier to accept was that I lost Dad when I was 12. I didn't have him as I got older like my siblings did. In some ways it was like growing up without a dad, if that makes any sense. Still, the man that I knew as my dad, wasn't. It was just so hard to make myself understand this was real, this was complicated, and this was heartbreaking.

There were so many things to think about and to consider, and I didn't even know where to begin. How could I possibly find out who my biological father was? Given that Mom was 41 when I was born, he would most likely, if he were still alive, be closer to 95 or better. Then I thought of Mom. Oh my gosh, what would people think of Mom? That thought haunted me for the longest time. I would never, ever want my mom painted in such a way that would make her look bad. Mom was a kind, gentle soul and those who knew her would agree. I didn't want her character to be tarnished in any way.

Nancy and I talked a lot over the next several months, trying to figure out who could possibly be my biological Father. I just kept saying, "This can't be true," but it WAS true. Nancy talked to me about different people that she knew that might fit the person, but it just didn't make any sense to me. Part of me wanted to know, but part of me didn't.

I really wanted to keep all this to myself and my siblings, at least for a while. I didn't feel right telling Mom's brother and sister, who were still living. What would they think of her? What would her other grandchildren think? This was just too much to think about. I just couldn't bear to tell anyone right now; I wasn't even sure I could tell anyone else EVER! I had literally just uncovered something that Mom took to her grave – if she even knew. This was way, way more than I ever could have imagined.

# DIGGING AND MORE DIGGING

After learning all this, I kept trying to figure out how Mom had met someone else. Mom didn't go anywhere to speak of, and when I was born, she very seldom drove. This was still so strange to me. Thinking back, I don't think I was ever angry; I think I was mostly just confused. Did Mom even know that the child she was carrying didn't belong to the man I knew as my dad? If Mom did know, did she ever tell anyone?

When I was growing up, since I was more than ten years younger than my next sibling, Dan, I would get teased about being the milkman's kid. Mom would say she didn't think she would have any more kids, and she was using birth control. Another thing that had been mentioned was how

I ended up with brown eyes. Both Mom and Dad had blue eyes. That question I always thought had an easy answer since Dad's siblings all had brown eyes, so that just skipped him, and I got them instead. All my siblings have blue eyes. I was the singular brown-eyed girl.

I started sizing up sibling genetics. Heights, eyes, anything I could think of. Mom wasn't very tall; we would tell her all the time she was 4'12". Dad was about 6'2. My brothers are all about average height, just under 6' or so, and Nancy is probably about 5'6. Me, I'm all of 5'2" – on a good day. When I was younger, I thought I really took after Mom in the height category.

Thinking about all these things and now knowing I had a different biological Father I started to wonder… What did "he" look like? How tall was he? More importantly, if he were still alive and I found out who he was, would I be able to meet him? Did he know about me? Did or do I have other siblings? The thoughts and questions kept increasing. I couldn't keep this out of my head and would think about it so much. The emotions were overwhelming at times.

One thing was certain; it wasn't going to change who I was. My family was and still is my family. My brothers and sister are still my brothers and sister. All the nieces and nephews are still that. The man that raised me until I was 12 was still my dad, and while I didn't get many years to have him on this earth, I knew he loved me, and that was all that mattered.

# STARTING A NEW JOURNEY

I was going to do whatever it took to possibly find out who 'he' was. So, I went back to 23andMe. I thought Natalie, the one who had done some of her own family's genealogy, might be able to help. This was in February of 2019. I wrote to her and told her what I had learned.

*Hi, Natalie, I know it's been a little bit since we've messaged, but I have a little more on what my family has found on the DNA testing. My sister and nephew had both submitted their DNA and we've learned that I am a half-sister (half-sibling) between the 5 of us. I am the youngest of the children (57) and two of our siblings have passed away. So now that I have a little more information for this... my search is on to find who might be my biological father. Chances are, they might also be deceased, but since your DNA and a few others do not cross with my sister's DNA, I'm guessing this is where the connection to you might be. Do you know or have any idea of anyone that might have been in Kentucky during the 1960s? I know this is a bit of a stretch, but any light you could share would be great. If you would like to email or call me, that would be great also. I appreciate anything you could share!*

She had given me her phone number and we ended up talking about her family. 23andMe says she and I are second cousins. This means that we most likely share the same great-grandparents. Natalie was very helpful and gave me a list of names to start with. I told her that I had been in contact with Mary Lou also, and how she had been a big help. They were both excited at the fact that I finally had some answers. But now, more questions needed answered.

At this point, I still hadn't really told anyone about what I had found out, with the exception of Nancy and Dan. In the beginning I was just trying to come to terms with all of this and would always worry about what people would think. I didn't want my mom thought of negatively. Besides, there was really no way to know what had happened. Was this a consensual relationship? Different questions were always on my mind.

I used all the available websites that I could find. I just couldn't find anything that would match up. So many years had gone by that it became harder to locate people. Would I ever find out anything? I felt like it was a never-ending loop.

A month or so later, I saw an advertisement on the My Heritage website where you could talk to a genealogist who could help with your DNA and any other questions you might have. I thought this might be worth looking into. For $100.00 I would get about 45 minutes to speak with someone. I was willing to do anything that could shed some light on this, and it turned out to be the best $100 I had ever spent!

# GENEALOGY LESSONS

I made my appointment to speak to a genealogist. Wow, was that an eye opener for sure! I spent about an hour with her. She sent me a link to where she could see my computer and then looked at my test results and those who I connected to. It was the most informative talk to date about all of this. I explained a little about what I had found out, told her I was now on a mission to find out all I could, and hopefully I could find out who my biological father was. She told me that it wasn't surprising – these types of calls were not that uncommon. During our call, she looked at the chromosome matches, the centimorgans, all of it. She went into detail about what the chromosome matches meant and how the matches factor into play on each chromosome. It was truly fascinating information. I could have talked to her for hours!

She saw the one I matched the most to was Mary Lou at 10.5%. Then she saw the others with lesser amounts. My sister, nephew, and those matches. I don't remember her name, but she went into detail about X and Y chromosomes and how they are passed down between male and female. She told me that Mary Lou and I shared an amount not always seen with that percentage. She said we were most likely first cousins. That information was helpful for me. The lady told me that with the other sites that I had used, I had a good start getting names to begin investigating with. I told her that Mary Lou and I had spoken a few times in the past while trying to match up surnames.

Then the bomb drops. She explained, "Well, if you can go back on her family tree and find her grandmother, then look at any male children her grandmother gave birth to, one of those are most likely going to be your biological father.

*What?* I slightly freaked out…

I sat in stunned silence at the computer. This lady had just told me how to find my biological Father.

"Wow, just like that?" I asked her.

"Yep," she said. "Your link to your biological dad's family will be through her. You've got a good start in finding this out. You're fortunate that you have amassed the amount of information that you have. A lot of people don't have that much information at this point." That made me feel a bit better about trying to figure out all this. I finished the conversation with her while still in a state of bewilderment. But at least now I had 'something' to go on. I was on a mission now for sure. I was going to find this person and learn who 'he' was.

# PUZZLE PIECES

I gathered all my information and reached out to Mary Lou and Natalie again. I owe a lot to each of them. They didn't know me from Adam, but they were so helpful, and when I had a question, I was able to contact them and they were there. Whenever I had an opportunity, I was on the computer looking up records, and anything I could find that might show something.

A month or so later, I was talking to Natalie on the phone. We continued to talk about all the information I got from the genealogist. I was telling her that I had used the link she had given me for her family tree on Ancestry so I could do all my digging for information. I told her how, in the beginning, I was just using this to build our family tree for fun and to get any medical information I could for our family. I had mentioned that I had a bleeding disorder and wondered where in my family it might have come from. I had always assumed it came from my dad's side of the family since Mom's side didn't have any issues with this that we knew of.

Natalie was a nurse so she asked me, "Do you have Von Willebrand's disease?" I explained that it was more of a platelet disorder.

"Do you lack a protein?" she asked.

I explained to her that it's more that my platelets don't function like they should. I have enough of them, they just don't work like they are supposed to. They lack the ability to form clots.

"That's what my son has!" she said.

"Oh my gosh, you're kidding me!" I replied.

"Well, there's the answer to where that genetic link came from," I told her. The doctor had explained to me that it was genetic, and now I knew. I finally had an answer to something. *It was on Dad's side of the family,* I thought, *just not the Dad I had figured it was!*

Whenever I had the chance, I was back to trying to find records. I previously mentioned all the websites that were so helpful in gathering family tree history. I finally had some names from Natalie's family tree to go on to use on the sites. There were so many children! *Oh my gosh,* I told myself, *this is going to take forever!*

I ended up going back to the FamilySearch website. There were more records there that I hadn't found on the other sites. Over the next several weeks, I took a name to see what records I could find. There were just so many dead ends. Nothing, nothing, nothing.

One day, while on the FamilySearch website, I realized I had checked all the names but wasn't finding anything, so I just started clicking on names on Natalie's ancestry account. I clicked on any woman that had male children.

I later realized that Mary Lou and I are first cousins once removed, which had added to the difficulty in finding matches.

One day I found a marriage license to a couple married in Louisville. *Finally something, but does this couple know my parents?* I asked myself.

The couple was married in the early 40s. He was in the service, so I figured he was most likely stationed at Ft. Knox. My parents were never around Ft. Knox, so this didn't really tie back to any connection between them that I knew of. I wasn't even sure if this was who I was looking for. I checked with Nancy to make sure Mom or Dad didn't have any connections to Ft. Knox. There were none that she knew of.

After looking at all the names on Natalie's ancestry account, no other name really took me anywhere. I wondered where I should go with this couple who were married in Louisville. The address listed on the marriage certificate wasn't even in the same area of town that my parents lived in.

Remember, on this site, if you upload information you can attach your contact information to attest that what you are adding is correct. I saw an email address so I thought, *What the heck? I'll email this person and see if they would be willing to help me in my search.*

# QUESTIONS AND ANSWERS

It was now May of 2019. I sent an email to the person that was attached to the record on file, and this is what I wrote:

*Hello,*

*I have recently done DNA testing, and I know this sounds strange, but I have learned that I have a biological father out there that I didn't know existed. I live in the Louisville, Kentucky area, and know that I am a descendant of the Bell family from Louisiana. I had talked to a genealogist who thought I might be related to the daughters of William Bell. After a little digging, I see that there is a Lester Rownd who is the son of Irene Bell (sister of William Bell). I saw he was married in Louisville, Kentucky; I'm following a hunch to see if this could be him. My mother was born in 1919 and died in 2011. We never knew anything of this, so I'm just trying to see what we could possibly find. Do you know if Lester lived in the Louisville area for very long? I see he was in the military, so I'm assuming he was stationed at Ft. Knox. This might not even be the connection I'm looking for, but I'm looking at all possibilities.*

*If you would like to email me or even talk, that would be great! I would appreciate any information you could provide.*

I ended by adding my name, phone number and email address. I thought maybe I would be lucky and hear something back from them.

I got in my car and went to my flute lesson. That was something I got from Mom – her love of music. I love playing the flute. I played all through school then didn't play again for 25 years or more. I started playing again about 12 years prior and realized how much I really missed it. I play at my church and with a local community concert band, and I'm even taking lessons from the person I took lessons from years ago.

Some 20 minutes later, when I was almost to the studio, my phone rang… It was from Georgia. I didn't know anyone in Georgia, so I thought it was probably a spam call, but I answered it anyway.

"Hello?"

"Hello," said the caller. "Are you Shari?" I told him I was, and the caller said, "Well, I'm the one you emailed on the FamilySearch website… (Dang, that was fast!).

My heart rate jumped up about 100 beats a minute. "Oh, hi! Thank you for calling me back! I know it's all strange information that I sent to you."

He told me his name was Van. He was very polite. He proceeded to tell me how his family had lived in Louisville for a short time, between 1957-1961, living in the Fern Creek area of town. His dad was in the Army, but they didn't live on base. He fought in WWII and was given an on-field promotion, with the rank of Captain, and later retired as a Major. We talk for about 20 minutes or so. The whole time I'm talking to him, nothing made a connection to my parents. We didn't live in Fern Creek and had nothing in common with Ft. Knox. I thought it was going to be another dead end.

I told him that everything I'd found so far didn't make a connection to my parents, but this was the only link I could find of anyone in the Louisville area. My parents never really went anywhere.

The gentleman told me how he was a teen when they lived in Louisville, and he was a golf caddie around that area of town. My parents didn't play golf either. We talked about horses and places around town that he would go to. He fondly remembered his early life in Louisville and talked a lot about the town. I was impressed by his memories of things which seemed like so long ago, but nothing connected. Nothing. I was feeling defeated yet again.

"I really appreciate you calling me back, and I hate that we couldn't find anything to make a connection," I said to him. He wished me luck in my search and I thanked him.

Just before we hung up I said, "I know this is a real stretch and might even seem silly, but by chance did your parents bowl?"

"As a matter of fact, my dad did," he said.

...His dad bowled!

Whoa. My hair stood up on my head. "Where did he bowl?" I asked.

"I believe it was called Poplar Level Lanes."

If I hadn't been sitting down in my car, I would have fainted. I know I would have fainted. I was just about to hang up, but something told me to ask him about bowling. What are the odds of me asking such a vague question?

"Well," I said, "looks like that's a big connection to my mom as she bowled and worked there." He was surprised. "When did you all leave Louisville?" I asked. He told me that his dad was transferred to Georgia in January of 1961. The timeframe certainly fit, as I was born in March of 1961. He went on to tell me that his dad bowled a few nights a week, so he went with him frequently.

I was just blown away by hearing all this information. I kind of laughed and told him, "Well, it might be premature to say, but I guess it's possible that you just might be my half-brother!"

"It wouldn't surprise me," he said.

"I guess we'll have a lot of discussions and learn all sorts of things," I told him. I asked if I could call him back when I had more time to talk, and he said of course. He told me that his parents were deceased; his dad had passed away in 1985. So 'if' he were my biological father, I wouldn't get to meet him, unfortunately.

After I got home that night, I sat and thought about it all, about how just building a family tree then doing DNA came to all this. I wondered what had gone on in my mom's life that caused this to happen. I was still in a state of shock about all I'd learned.

I talked to my husband that night and told him that I had spoken to the man that could possibly be my half-brother. He was so supportive through this whole thing and was happy that I had finally found the connection I'd been looking for. "I knew you would eventually find what you needed to find. You put your mind to this and were determined to get some answers. I knew you weren't going to give up."

I called both Nancy and Dan that night. I told them I had spoken to someone who had given me a lot of information and who I thought may have just given me the biggest lead of all. I told them about the email I sent, asking for information then getting a call back. I told them that after explaining everything and finding the connections that fit to Mom, there was a chance that he might be my half-brother. My sister said she had thought it might have been possible that it would have been someone she might have known, but that didn't appear to be the case, as the name didn't sound familiar at all. Dan told me that he was happy to hear that a missing piece of the puzzle may have finally been solved.

After I talked to Nancy and Dan, I thought about the past few months. After all the searching, it was now possible that I had finally found that link. It was still so surreal to think about. What if Mom had still been alive when I found all this out? The questions just kept popping up in my mind.

Later that night, I went and got out some pictures of my parents. There weren't a lot of them, but I looked at them and wondered if Dad knew. Was this some deep dark secret that was never told? I remembered all the things said to me as a kid about the eye color, the milkman's kid comments, etc.

I didn't want to seem overzealous to Van and ask question after question, but my curiosity was about to get the best of me. Over the next few weeks, we talked about different things, and he told me he'd be willing to take a DNA test. I would take another one also, both using Ancestry. The DNA websites aren't willing to just let you upload your information to another site, and since he already had an account with Ancestry it made sense to do so.

I got to thinking to myself, *If Van 'is' my half-brother, what does he look like? Do I look like this family? Does Van have any siblings?* I needed to calm my nerves and my mind, and not get ahead of myself. I just needed to wait for the results to come back.

# COINCIDENCES?

While waiting for the test results to come back, Van and I talked about so many things. His dad was from Louisiana, and I had told him how I had DNA matches to people from there. He knew of the people I had matched to. I kind of think at this point we probably both knew we were going to match as half-siblings but were still waiting for that confirmation.

Van and his wife, Claudette, live in a small town in Georgia, near South Carolina. He has two sons who both live in Georgia too. He has a sister who lives in Georgia and a brother who had passed away.

I told him about my parents and siblings. Van is about 15 years older than me. I told him how a lot of my siblings were in the bowling center quite frequently when they were younger. When Van told me how old he was, I told him that he and my brother Dan quite possibly played as kids back then. Our conversations were very informative, and it seemed easy to talk to him.

One evening while I was talking to Van, Eddie asked, "Why don't you send him a picture of your mom to see if he recognizes her?" I told Van I was going to send him a picture of my mom, one of her on her 90th birthday since I didn't have one readily available of her in her 40s.

He got the picture of my Mom and immediately said, "I remember her!"

"What?! You do?!"

He replied, "Oh yes, I would have remembered her no matter her age. She was always so nice to me as a kid at the bowling center. She always brought me popcorn and a Coke while my dad was bowling."

I couldn't believe it. Wow. Mom loved kids, so I could certainly see her doing that.

In another conversation we had, he explained to me that he and his wife are Mormon and how they like to visit temples in other cities and that they had visited the one in Louisville. Not knowing much about the Mormon faith, I said, "Oh, that's interesting! Where about in Louisville is it?" He tells me it's in Crestwood, just outside of Louisville.

"Van, that temple is probably less than a mile from where I live. You most likely drove past my house to go visit it."

"Well, that's something, isn't it?" he said. This is crazy!

Van has a background in IT and is retired from a large computer company. He told me that because of his background in IT, he had helped with the FamilySearch website. His family tree is very well mapped out and full of detailed information. Then it hit me – this was why it was possible to find the marriage certificate!

I was still so curious to see what Van's family looked like. I thought back on it, and I had never thought I looked much like the dad who raised me, other than having the brown eyes like his brothers and sisters. That was about it. I had

Mom's height and some features but to say I really "look" like my mom, I would have said no.

Right before our test results came back, I asked Van if he had any pictures of his dad. He said he would have to do some digging around to find some, but he would send me one. His dad's family grew up in the Louisiana Bayou and there weren't a lot of pictures taken back then. After we finished talking, Van found his parents' wedding picture taken in 1942 and sent me a screenshot. I looked at his parents then zoomed in on his dad. I literally gasped.

"What's wrong?" Eddie asked. I turned the phone around to show him. He looks right at me and says, "That's your dad. Make no mistake on that. You don't need a DNA test to prove that." The resemblance was incredible. The eyes, the shape of his face, the brow line, all of it. I cried.

It was true, this was my biological Father.

I called Van back and told him, "I don't think I need a confirmation of a DNA test to tell me – I'm very certain he is my biological Father. I just can't get over the resemblance."

My biological father, me again after Ashley was born (1987), me at my high school graduation

Van sent me a picture of him and told me that he looks more like his mom's side of the family but that he thinks his sister looks more like their dad's side. I sent him pictures of me; one of me when I was younger and one more recent. He saw the resemblance too. I told him that it had been a lot to absorb, but it was exciting to now know that I might have more family out there that I never known about! Through our conversations, I had gotten the feeling that he was also excited at the possibility of having another sibling.

Around the end of May of 2019 we got our results back.Van and I share 1,601 centimorgans across 32 segments of DNA, which is a 99% match that we were half-siblings. He called me as soon as he got his results. "Well hello, sister!" he said.

I said, "Hello, brother!" The feeling was incredible; I don't even know how to explain it. I have more family! A brother and sister, and nieces and nephews. It really hit me at that point, and I was overcome with emotions. There were more tears, but this time it was happy tears.

I called Nancy and Dan to let them know that our results showed that Van and I are half-siblings. They were so happy for me. I told them how Van remembered Mom from when he was a teen at the bowling center, and the connections through his church quite possibly helped me find the information I had been looking for.

Over the next few weeks we worked to set up a time when we could meet. My husband was due to have hip replacement surgery, and Van needed to get his schedule opened as well.

I was still undecided about whether I should tell other family members what I had discovered. Did it really matter, or should I just be upfront with all of it? I decided that I would just keep this to those few who did know, at least for a while. Maybe after I was able to meet Van and let everything sink in I would let others know.

# ALL ABOUT FAMILY, NEW AND OLD

After getting our schedules cleared, we made plans to meet. In July of 2019, Van and his wife Claudette made the drive from Georgia to Kentucky. I was nervous and excited at the same time. We agreed to meet at a local restaurant for dinner. It would be me, Eddie, my daughter Ashley, and Dan and his wife Patricia (Trish). We all pretty much arrived at the restaurant at the same time. I saw a car with Georgia plates and figured that must be them. All the months of searching and the emotional roller-coaster after finding all this out, and now there we were. It was really happening. My heart was racing with anticipation.

"Hello Van", I said, "It's nice to finally meet my brother!"

"And I gained a sister too," he replied. The anxiety just seemed to dissipate after that. Over the next few hours we talked, and Van told us a lot about his family, growing up in an Army family, etc. Van was in the Army for a while too, and his other brother, Raymond (who had passed away), had been in the Air Force. As I sat there during our dinner, I was thinking how surreal it was. It was just incredible to think about and absorb it all.

Van had brought many pictures of his family and showed them to us all. There were pictures of his dad (my biological Father), and other members of my now new family.

While we were all chatting, Ashley was looking through photos on her own. In one of the photos there was a group of people, but one person caught her attention. Ashley tapped me on the shoulder and said, "Mom, this little girl looks a lot like you did when you were a little girl, don't you think?" I took the photo from her hands, looked at it and thought to myself, wow, she really does look like me as a child!

I asked, "Hey, Van, could I ask you who the little girl in this photo is?"

Van took the photo from me and looked at it for a second. He looked up at me with a smile and said, "That's my little sister, Lynn." Ashley and I looked at each other with a little laugh.

Ashley said, "There you have it – that's why you look so much alike! That's your sister too!" The resemblance really was uncanny. Seeing that photo just brought everything full circle. I thought back to my childhood and how I thought I never really looked like the siblings I had known my whole life. There I looked at a picture of a little girl who I'm told is my half-sister and see how much I look like her. For the first time, I can actually see how much I really look like one of my siblings.

Lee, my half-sister Lynn, and myself

Van and his wife stayed in town for a few days. I took them to where he used to live, and we drove over to where Poplar Level Lanes used to be. It had closed several years before, but the building was still there. Van remembered it all. His memory is impeccable. It was truly an incredible visit. We made plans for Eddie and I to go to Georgia soon to visit with him, meet his kids and my half-sister.

Over the next few months, and after discussing this with Eddie, Nancy and Dan, I decided that I would tell the rest of the family what I had learned. Things were all confirmed, so there was really no reason not to tell them. I was just so worried about what people would think. Trish had told me that what's in the past is done and that it doesn't matter anymore. It was nobody's business; we don't know the circumstances of why, and it's not relevant anymore anyway. She was right.

Slowly, one by one, I called my family. Each one learning that I had a different biological Father was nothing short of complete shock. Most everyone never knew of Mom and Dad's relationship prior to me being born, it was just so long ago. I laughed and told them," You just never know when building a family tree, there could be circumstances to cause the addition of another branch; and here we are." After telling the story to everyone, it was a relief of sorts. All agreed that it didn't matter what had happened in the past – it was all about going forward at that point.

I had called and talked to my Aunt Phyl, who was Mom's younger sister. After I told her everything, I asked her if Mom had ever confided to her about anything in her life. No, nothing she'd said. She told me that Mom was a very private person, and the fact that she lived so far away probably added to Mom not sharing much with her.

I then talked to Mom's sister-in-law, Aunt Dee Dee, and asked her the same thing. She didn't really know anything either but said that some of the family on Mom's side had always wondered why I didn't resemble any of my siblings. I just laughed and said, "Now we know why!" All that time nothing was ever said. I thought that was so funny.

Finally, the rest of the family knew the whole story. Many were shocked, of course, but were very happy that after all the searching I had done I was able to find the other part of my biological family. It was still unbelievable that Mom had never said a word to anyone, if she knew, at least not to anyone we could ever ask.

Me and Van at our first meeting – July 2019

# FIRST IMPRESSIONS

In November of 2019, right after Thanksgiving Eddie and I went to Georgia to see Van, Claudette, and Van's sons. Eddie and I drove to a small town in Georgia, close to the South Carolina border where Van lives. After the first day of visiting, we all jumped in our rental and drove about 2 ½ hours to his son's house just north of Atlanta.

I think I would be correct in saying when we meet people for the first time, we want to make a nice impression. I wanted Van and Claudette to be comfortable meeting me for the first time, and me going to Georgia was no different. I guess it's normal to have nerves or excitement overwhelm you in situations like this. On the way to Georgia, I wondered how I would be received when meeting more of my new family. Should I have anything to worry about? What if they didn't like me? There was a lot to think about. For the most part, I was comfortable with it though. Van had told me a lot about his sons, and I was genuinely looking forward to meeting everyone.

Van has two sons, Chris and William (Will). We were going to Will's house, and my half-sister Lynn would be there later, bringing pictures with her.

We left for Will's house and were about 15 to 20 minutes from arriving when I started to feel queasy. I had been turning around in my seat to talk to Van and Claudette a lot, and sometimes I get a little motion sickness from doing that. So I focused on the road in front of me while Eddie drove, but it just kept getting worse. Finally, I told him to pull over, I was going to be sick. Eddie pulled over and I proceeded to lose my breakfast in a parking lot. I tell you, I was mortified. There was my new brother and sister-in-law, and I was out there throwing up. It's not like you can help it, but I felt awful about it. Eddie was there for me, and I just wanted to cry. Everyone was so sweet about it, so I told them I knew it was motion sickness and that I would be ok.

We finally arrived at Will's house. He and his wife Jenny were the best hosts. It was a beautiful sunny November day.

"Wow!" Will said, "I finally get to meet my new aunt! I see so much resemblance in your eyes."

I said, "Yes, I see that a lot from the pictures I've seen."

"It's great to have you here to meet everyone. We have so much to catch up on." I can't even describe how comfortable I felt there.

I met everyone who was there and we all sat down to eat pizza. I didn't want to upset my stomach, so I just had something to drink. A few minutes later, I felt that queasiness again. I was thinking to myself, this can't be happening – again. Oh, but it did. I looked at Eddie and told him I was going to get sick again. I was so embarrassed. There was a bathroom at the front of the house. So then I was in the bathroom of a house I had literally just walked into 30 minutes ago, getting sick again. I kept apologizing to them, and Jenny was so sweet and kind about the whole thing.

"It's totally ok," she told me. "Don't even worry about this!" I didn't understand how or why I was sick. I wasn't nervous or anxious about meeting everyone; in fact, I felt pretty calm about the whole thing.

Will, me and Chris – my new nephews

Eddie and Will went to a store not far from the house to get me something to settle my stomach. At this point I was thinking it wasn't motion sickness but something I must have eaten at breakfast. They brought back something for my stomach, and I took it. But that didn't work, and about 20 minutes later, you guessed it – I visited that same bathroom. That was quite a memorable first impression that none of us will ever forget!

A little while later, Lynn and her husband Danny came over. By this time I was resting on a couch in the back of the house. I felt like I had just ruined the whole day. I didn't really get to talk much to Lynn or her husband, or share any of the pictures that we both had brought. Then Van's other son, Chris, had to leave too, so I didn't really get a chance to talk much with him either.

Will and Jenny made us feel so welcome and told me not to worry about anything. The entire time I was thinking, *How in the world could this happen?* It's something we can all laugh about now, but at that moment I couldn't find a rock big enough to crawl under!

Me and my half-sister, Lynn

We stayed for a few more hours then had to get back to where Van lives. While it wasn't the visit I had anticipated, it was still great to meet more of my family. I was told that I reminded them of Aunt Dorothy, who is my biological father's sister. I told them I would love to see a picture of her, and Van said he would see what he could do to find one.

We stayed in Georgia for another day then started our way back home. Will even texted me to see how I was doing then made jokes about the whole eventful day. We plan on staying in touch and since no one is that far away, we'll make more visits in the future. There's a lot to catch up on!

On the way home I told Eddie that it was incredible how this whole thing had played out, and how things all came together. I'm sure there are many people out there who, like me, have found out they have a different parent that they never knew about. Every situation is different, and while some end well, I'm sure there are some that don't. I'm very fortunate to have a family that was just as excited to meet me as I was them. What started out as just building a family tree turned my world completely upside down and ended with more than I could have ever imagined. The emotions, tears, anticipations – all of it has brought me a new branch of my family. I'm so blessed.

# NEW BRANCHES AND NEW BEGINNINGS

When Van and I did our DNA match, I created an account with Ancestry too. There were new names that I matched to that were not on 23andme. I asked Van about them, and one is a first cousin – the son of my biological aunt. Van explained that the cousin is what some people call a double cousin. Siblings (brother and sister) from one family married siblings (sister and brother) from another family. The aunt ended up living in and around the Louisville area.

I told him I understood that, as Eddie's parents had a similar situation – sisters from one family married brothers from another family.

In June of 2020, I decided to reach out to the cousin that I matched to on Ancestry. I introduced myself and explained the short version of how I came to be a part of this new family. I told him that if given the chance, I'd love to talk to or possibly meet him one day.

I did a search on the name to see if I could learn any details. Sadly, I discovered that he had passed away at the beginning of the year. That was really disheartening. I had really hoped to have had the chance to meet him. I read his obituary and saw that he had lived here in town. I read further down, and it mentioned that he had retired from a company that my brother Dan had worked at and is also retired from. I called Dan and asked if he had ever heard of this person and he said the name sounded familiar. I saw a picture attached to the obituary so I sent that to him. Dan told me, "Oh, I do remember him! We both worked in the IT Department for probably 20 years or so. Our cubicles were next to each other."

I couldn't believe what he had just said. "Dan, this guy is my biological first cousin!"

"What?!?" He laughed, "You're kidding me."

"No, and what are the odds? You worked next to this man for all those years and it turns out he's related to me." That was incredible.

I called Van to tell him what I had learned about our cousin. He hadn't known about his passing. Van told me that he thought Aunt Dorothy had passed a few years ago. I took it upon myself to see if I could find the children that were mentioned in the obituary. Through the powers of social media, I finally heard back from them, and the daughter told me that Aunt Dorothy, her grandmother, was still living in Texas. I told her about me and how I was related to the family after doing a DNA test. She was kind enough to send me a picture of her grandmother and her dad as a young boy. I could really see how we resembled one another. I looked at the pictures and thought about how amazing it all was. There were so many little twists that have entwined this whole thing. The coincidental connections, and just getting on different genealogy sites brought me where we are today.

For me, in the grand scheme of things, nothing has really changed though. I could sit and ponder the what if's... Did Mom know or not? Honestly, that doesn't even matter anymore. My gut feeling is maybe not in the beginning, but as I got older, I think she probably did, and for whatever reason she chose to keep it to herself. But I am still Charles' daughter. He loved me dearly, even though his time on earth with me was short. The family that I have known all my life is still my family. That's no different. When people discover through DNA that they have different parents or family – it's a situation that could go either way. I think that's one of the reasons I chose to share my story. DNA and genealogy have opened a Pandora's box, if you will, for many people – and inside that box are discoveries that have done everything from solving unsolved mysteries to freeing wrongly convicted prisoners. It can also open those discoveries that we're not able to understand or accept.

I have been very fortunate to say that my discoveries have been wonderful. It was a lot to absorb, and many, many times my emotions were overwhelming. But I'm really looking forward to building a relationship with my newly discovered family. This new branch of my family tree has now been completed.

# A FINAL CHAPTER - BUT NOT THE END...

In the summer of 2020, things were very uncertain given that Covid-19 was spreading all over the place. Before things got really bad, Eddie and I managed a short visit down to Georgia. We were able to spend a few days getting to see Van and Claudette then over to visit with Will and Jenny. It was great to spend a few days seeing them and doing more catching up from all the past years we'd missed out on. We made tentative plans for them to come up to Louisville the following year in hopes of them meeting my family that live here. How amazing that would be for everyone to meet.

That fall, I wrote to 23andme and thanked them for helping me in my discovery. Their website plus talking to the genealogist brought me to find the biological family I never knew about. One of their public relations spokespersons reached out to me, wanting to hear my story and get to know more about me. We did a video call and ended up talking for about 45 minutes. She was happy to hear that my story had a good outcome. I told her that it was my goal for the next summer to have my Georgia family come here to meet my Louisville family. She passed my name to their media company and asked if I would mind speaking to them about my story.

In the spring of 2021, we were able to get a summer cookout planned for June. I was really thrilled that both sides of my family would finally get to meet! My sister Nancy and her family from North Carolina would be coming too. I had reached back out to 23andme and told them that the families would be meeting in the middle part of June. She was excited for me and asked if they could contact a local news station about our cookout. I told her yes, that would be great, although I never heard back from anyone – and that was fine too. I'm not comfortable talking to people in public, so speaking to a news station would have made my nerves a wreck!

Well, don't you know it, the day of the cookout a local news station called me and wanted to come out to do a story about me and my family. Wow! I was a complete wreck inside, but it honestly went so well. The news reporter spoke to me then to Van, and it's something that I will forever treasure. We shared more stories and pictures, and my family members were so excited to meet my new family.

It was the most beautiful day; the weather cooperated, the sun shone bright, and it was a great day for a gathering. My heart was so full. All in all, there were over 40 people here. It was amazing, everyone was in awe of how this had all come together, and Van told me how much he enjoyed getting to meet everyone. While talking to Van, he mentioned how he had never had the opportunity to have family reunions. He had been to family reunions, but not his own family's. I told him that he was now part of this family and that we would be having future cookouts and family get-togethers, which we love to do! I told him that he hadn't seen anything yet; wait until he met Eddie's side of the family. That cookout is easily over 100 people since he comes from a very large family.

My sister Lynn and her family, and my nephew Chris were not able to make this cookout, but we've already planned a cookout for next summer so hopefully they will be here to meet everyone then.

Early in the fall of 2021, we took a vacation and made a stop in Georgia for a visit. It's nice that it's not terribly far away and that we're able to make a relatively short drive to visit. It was during this visit that Van and I were able to meet our cousin, Natalie, who I mentioned previously. Van and Natalie had talked to each other about genealogy years before knowing about me, but they had never actually met. Natalie had helped me so much in gathering research about the people who I would eventually come to know as my new family. It was amazing to finally have all three of us meet for the first time.

Here is my wish – that there are more family cookouts, more gatherings, and that we're able to make more memories. I'm thankful beyond comprehension.

# ABOUT THE AUTHOR

Shari Klosterman put her first time writing, *My Family Tree – Taken to the Grave,* to work after discoveries in her own family tree. After years of studying genealogy and building her own family tree, she took her information and found family mysteries that went well beyond what she ever imagined.

Shari is from Crestwood, Kentucky and has been married for 11 years to her husband Ed, and has a daughter, three bonus children, and five grandchildren. Besides doing family trees, she is an accomplished bowler, plays the flute, enjoys photography and, in the summertime, you'll find her out in her 2014 Mustang GT California Special.

"Building my family tree was fun and exciting. With many free sites available and some at a minimal cost, the potential discoveries that you could find are worth it – you just don't know who you might be related to!"

Made in the USA
Monee, IL
10 January 2023

25017340R00073